Steady Daylight

Steady Daylight

POEMS

JOSEPH BATHANTI

Louisiana State University Press
BATON ROUGE

Published by Louisiana State University Press
lsupress.org

Copyright © 2026 by Joseph Bathanti
All rights reserved. Except in the case of brief quotations used in articles or reviews, no part of this publication may be reproduced or transmitted in any format or by any means without written permission of Louisiana State University Press.

LSU Press Paperback Original

Designer: Kaelin Chappell Broaddus
Typefaces: Bunyan Pro, text; Apotek, display

Cover photograph: *Sunlight*, by Huck Beard. Used with permission of Huck Beard.

Grateful acknowledgment is extended to the editors of the following journals, in which the poems listed, in some cases in different versions, first appeared: *Aethlon: The Journal of Sport Literature*: "Little League"; *Appalachian Lit*: "Promotion"; *Asheville Poetry Review*: "Baby," "Prince Street," and "Wedding Soup"; *Hollins Critic*: "The Feast of San Mauro"; *Journal of American Medicine*: "Wisdom"; *Litmosphere*: "Catharsis"; *The Midnight Oil*: "Sucker Punch"; *Paterson Poetry Review*: "The Cellar," "No Use Kicking," and "Shouldering It"; *Pittsburgh Quarterly*: "Larimer Field"; *Presence: A Journal of Catholic Poetry*: "CiCi's," "Prince Street," and "Requiem for the Living"; *Plume*: "Omega Street," "A Pittsburgh Bakery in Winter," "The Raccoon," "Taking It Back," and "Ubi Sunt"; *Red Dirt Forum*: "Excommunication"; *RSAJournal (Rivista di Studi American)*: "Zippo"; *The Sun*: "Right Guard" and "Steady Daylight"; *VIA: Voices in Italian Americana*: "Shrovetide" and "Strike"; *Vox Populi*: "Steady Daylight."

Many thanks also to the editors of the following anthologies, in which the poems listed, in some cases in different versions, appeared: *Crossing the Rift: North Carolina Poets on 9/11 and Its Aftermath*: "Katy"; *Keystone Poetry: Contemporary Poets on Pennsylvania*: "Requiem for the Living"; *Live Encounters: American Poets and Writers*: "The First Time They Forget," "Mount Carmel," and "Singer"; *Shining Rock Poetry Anthology & Book Review*: "Requiem for the Living"; *The Gulf Tower Forecasts Rain: Pittsburgh Poems*: "The Feast of San Mauro" and "A Pittsburgh Bakery in Winter."

Cataloging-in-Publication Data are available from the Library of Congress.

ISBN 978-0-8071-8585-8 (pbk.: alk. paper) — ISBN 978-0-8071-8624-4 (pdf) — ISBN 978-0-8071-8623-7 (epub)

CONTENTS

I.
DING DANG DONG

Omega Street 3
Zippo 6
Singer 8
Prince Street 10
Baby 13

II.
THE CRUEL WORLD

Little League 19
Promotion 21
Cici's 23
Larimer Field 24
Shrovetide 28
Taking It Back 29
Strike 33
Sucker Punch 34
Excommunication 35
The Cellar 37
Jeanne-Marie 40

III.
MANOVALE

No Use Kicking   45

Catharsis   47

Wisdom   50

Shouldering It   52

Basic Oxygen   56

IV.
ASPETTARE

The Raccoon   61

Mount Carmel   63

Extreme Unction   65

Right Guard   68

The First Time They Forget   71

A Pittsburgh Bakery in Winter   72

Katy   74

Wedding Soup   77

Ubi Sunt   79

V.
CODA

Requiem for the Living   85

Steady Daylight   87

The Feast of San Mauro   91

PART I

Ding Dang Dong

Underneath, the street is brick,
brick that is no longer whole and
red, but chipped and gray like
the faces of dead people trapped
under lava. The street heaves up
bricks, the guts of the street spit
up brick. The face of the street
cracks open and reveals its belly of
brick, the gray faces.

—Tina De Rosa, *Paper Fish*

Omega Street

The crosshairs of East Liberty,
the shaved sight, the true bead,
like an M-16, is the *cruci*
Booze Alley slashes

from Larimer Avenue through Omega Street
where handsome Emory,
the light-skinned *refined* negro boy
my Marseillais grandmother,

Suzanne Marisse, dotes on,
reads Countee Cullen on his stoop;
and my *Napolitano* tailor
grandfather, Luigi, paces, night

upon day, hands clasped behind him,
prickly serge waistcoat,
gray fedora, eyes to earth—
a sealed, silent vault.

In their wedding portrait,
he sits in wicker,
right hand caressing his left,
fingers fantastically long;

blazing collar, cravat, pouting lips,
locked jaw; in his lap,
a satin-banded homburg;
pomade waves black the brow.

I've tried not to think of my face
engendered by his, nor his little bed—
two sticks and the mutilated Nazarene
crossed on plaster at its head—

in the corner of my grandmother's boudoir,
sash wide to squalling snow,
feather four-poster, embroidered linen,
a dozen rosaries coiled at its pillow.

I've his brooding left eye,
half his mouth. In the frame,
Suzanne stands next to him,
illumined Vermeer visage,

open-throat white chemise, gloves,
no jewelry, a lone gardenia
pinned to her chapeau.
She conjures the future

and will not foreswear it.
I have her right eye, half her mouth.
They say she's of Syrian blood,
educated in convents across Europe

and Mesopotamia. Her father
engineered on the Suez Canal.
Photogravures portray her
flanked by bald Maasai women

in beaded collars. Before Luigi,
they say, she had a husband
who hanged himself in the cold
earthen cellar with the cheeses

above her locked dowry trunk.
The bathtub bloats in the cellar
where I shiver in the shadow
of the twirling cadaver of the past

while my grandmother scrubs me
with pumice, green clay soap from the Nile,
and sings *Frère Jacques.* Quaking,
the mummified coal furnace

drives its swollen ducts through the rafters
like Atlas assuming the world.
From the eight-story spires
of Saints Peter and Paul,

morning bells gong:
Sonnez les matines,
Ding Dang Dong,
Ding Dang Dong.

Zippo

At the corner of Larimer and Meadow
stands my mother in blue dotted Swiss,
square Pilgrim bib, lace-tatted, smirking
camellia in her long brown wavy hair;
my father in a cocoa double-breasted suit,
snap-brim fedora, white shirt,
California Satins necktie.

They've never met.
They have been placed here by God—
in the bleeding heart of East Liberty—
to lay eyes upon each other for the first time.
Of all those whelped, from Adam
and Eve into the fifth decade
of the twentieth century, they've arrived
this very moment foretold in writ
on the corner across from Genevieve's.

From inside his jacket pocket,
my father extracts a package of Camels
(*Turkish and domestic blend cigarettes*)
and breaks its blue seal
like canceled Moroccan postage:
the massive placid camel mooning
behind distant palms and pyramids,
a walled city crowned in mosques and minarets.

He ignites the first of twenty tailor-mades
with the silver Zippo I will come to love,
years later, studying him
at the kitchen table on Prince Street—
newspaper spread to appease my mother
treadling the Victorian Singer,
his wedding gift to her—

as he removes with a tiny screwdriver
the base of it, and fits the nozzle
of Red Devil's Lighter Fluid
to its cotton batting port.

On his little yellow tin—
from the Dome Chemical Company,
Cincinnati, Ohio—
the cartoon Diavolo brandishes his own lighter,
its flame arabesque, poised to immolate
a recent batch of the mortally sinful,
hurled off boxcars arrived in ghetto Gehenna—
my ultimate destination,
swears Sister Sarah, my first grade teacher.

Coal-black goatee,
beaked nose like a linoleum knife,
paunchy, with tiny breasts, he crams
like a sausage his red leotard,
red feather flaring
from his oily black Sicilian ringlets,
punctuated with two little hornlets—
almost cute—though he's deceit and torture:
DANGER—FLAMMABLE
HARMFUL OR FATAL IF SWALLOWED.
Keep out of the reach of children.

Singer

A wedding gift from my father,
my mother's sleek black Singer

stationed in the alcove on Prince Street.
Bedded twilight in rooms a floor above,

my sister and I listened to its steady thrum,
litany and lullaby, as my mother spun

the handwheel and fed it thread unraveling
from its spool skewered on the spindle,

spitting from the loaded bobbin,
another cartridge in reserve,

such speed the Singer smoked.
Its golden gothic signature scorched

into its mysterious arm, therein secreted
the *shaft, presser bar, faceplate.*

My mother paused for it to quell,
checked its belt and feed dog,

hand basted a cuff, slit and stitched
another buttonhole, pinned fabric

to a pattern, as if under a spell
to clothe us new come dawn.

The Singer hovered—mid-tack,
panting—then revved off again.

My mother's long brown hair
lifted in its wake. Past the night,

long after Marie and I faded into dream,
she traveled the scarce trestle of morning—

my father, chained to a boom crane,
building time on his sentence,

at the threshold of the troposphere,
stories over steel's open hearth—

thimbled fingers skirting the throat plate,
the needle but a micron from piercing her.

Prince Street

Out of clammy pajamas,
I twist, naked beneath the crucifix

trussed in brittle Easter palm
tied to my bed.

Black bugs worm the window screen,
tick about the night-light,

the bony carapace of my chest.
In ambush hovers July.

Night, in no hurry,
knows I fear sleep.

From the living room
below glows TV.

Mummy guards the house,
worried over Daddy pulling turns

at the mill, on a boom crane
above the Monongahela.

Sweating shadows smoke
cigarettes on my wall.

Headlights scour me:
the farewell murmur,

hush and velocity,
a car speeding Prince Street—

we rent in a brick row
next door to Marmo—

where hoodlums play chicken.
Across the hall sleeps

my untroubled sister, Marie.
She doesn't stir at impact—

the DeSoto hurtling eighty
into the four-story sycamore

that splits our sidewalk:
the surge and duration of sound,

compression waves, echoic
hiss and seizure of expiring belts

and armatures, the steady discharge
of fluids—tremble gives way

to black coils of silence—
prelude, portal to nightmare.

A boy has been terribly hurt:
He went through the windshield.

Stripping the blanket from my bed,
Mummy must keep him warm.

She must keep him awake.
Such a viciously hot night,

how can he be cold?
I climb in bed with Marie,

shake against her
as she says the rosary,

picturing *through the windshield*
a bloody boy-saint beatified in glass.

Baby

Parsimony was the curdle my mother
cut her accounts of the Depression with—
and nurtured in the inch of tepid water
permitted each night she bathed me,
then held my hand, called me *Pigeon*,
as shivering I scaled the lip of the tub
and fell into the soft towel
in which she wrapped me.

She obsessed over the meterman's creep
beneath our house to mark kilowatts,
scurried behind us, flicking off switches:
Your father doesn't work for Duquesne Light
(my father shoveled slag for U.S. Steel all night).
Food was plentiful, but wasting it sacrilege.
How would you like to go hungry?
To starve?
To live in the poorhouse?
She wasn't too proud to bend for a penny
on the scurvy floor of Booze Alley,
or buy *crippled* bread at Stagno's.
She could live a week off a thimble of chicory,
thread a needle in her sleep.

The youngest girl-child,
the one called *Baby*, but never babied,
my mother had slept in the same bed
between her two sisters, polenta—
which she never let past her teeth again—
every night of the Depression,
then the war: a brother in Burma;
another in Algiers; yet another,
an infant, laid out at home,
dead to pneumonia.

A lump of coal was no metaphor.
Mythic was the ragman,
the resigned clop of his dying draft mare
draying along Omega Street,
where ten of them lived in a stone house,
the size of a shoe—blood soup
bubbling oracularly in the black pot—
Baby's mother, bled, womb raked out
by the surgeon's knife, weeks abed,
linen laced with chaplets, writing letters
to Roosevelt's wife; her father,
slinking in, drunk, from Toto's,
pitching down the haunted cellar steps,
nostrils pumping fangs of blood,
someone whispering in my mother's ear:
Let the son of a bitch bleed to death.

But they had been clean—as anyone,
Thank God—spotless, immaculate.
My mother scraped and scraped,
boiled, scrubbed and punished:
counters, tables, walls, our clothes and faces.
She gaped wild-eyed as my sister and I ate,
as if a tornado might funnel the kitchen
and suck us into its maw;
or a Messerschmitt, with its deadly tonnage,
home in on our Prince Street rowhouse.
The enemy knew my father was at the mill.
The plane's bomb bay had opened.
People were saying things behind our back.

What is true? What happened?
I suppose I didn't care.
I just wanted to be left alone,
shed of *scrimp,* and *save.*

I craved more—two, three, ten, of everything.
My mother insisted: *Basta!* Enough.
I had you; you didn't have me, she often declared.
That much was true:
I was derivative, owned, possessed, *had*—
no past, the future but a livid cloud
one entered in good faith and scorn—
the yoke of ancestry, its blood-reckoning.

Noon, the air raid siren keened.
Slum dogs choked on their tongues.
Saints Peter and Paul's steeple tolled The Angelus.
Forced to my knees in the street,
I held an imaginary dagger to my heart.
Everywhere danger: gas chambers,
electric chairs, concentration camps, suicide.
An empty pop bottle yielded
a two-cent refund at CiCi's store,
but I loved smashing them
against the rent man's door.

PART II

The Cruel World

It is a love and a rage.
The love you already know about,
lurking in all the clichés about
ethnicity: pungent, generic. Like garlic,
it stays with you.

—Alane Salierno Mason, "Respect"

Little League

Spring in the cruel world—
the cruelest month.
In our flannels,

we open Little League season with a parade—
led from Saints Peter and Paul by Father Ott,
altar boys bearing processional crosses—

across Lincoln Avenue Bridge,
spanning Silver Lake, though no lake,
but a drive-in movie and Dairy Queen.

We march all the way to Paulson Field
and eat lasagna at the North Italian Club.
Nick Risorgimento gives a speech,

scarlet Sons of Columbus sash
splashed over his belly.
Broiled from the long walk,

then oozing ricotta,
a few kids throw up in the alley.
Victor Valdi's tongue freezes to a fudgesicle.

Frantic it will stick there forever, like a curse,
and East Liberty coin for him a mythic name—
Vittorio the Tongue, Victor Fudgesicle,

and he'll become the nightmare scourge of children,
like the *mostro, Spacaluccio,*
who resides beneath the bridge

spanning *Basa La Vallone*—
Vic shrieks and rips
the lolly stick from his mouth,

brandishes it like a fetish—
the dorsal layer of his tongue
in pink relief.

Promotion

It is tradition the Parish pastor,
Dietrich Ott, commend promotion,
the last day of school, to the next form.
Freeze-tag still, sick for the final bell,
the long, blessed bout of amnesia,
we wait for Ott's Roman collar,
spent stogie swagged to his lip.

He lives in the rectory with his maid,
comes and goes through the sacristy tunnel.
No one likes him, a German—
there's a grudge from the war;
we're reminded of it every day,
and the Depression—nor his homilies
from the pulpit about money.
My fabrications, during Confession,
put him to sleep. When he wakes
to confer absolution and penance—
Go in peace, and sin no more—
he says my name, first and last,
exploding the myth of anonymity.

Strapped to my skinny wrist,
the tiny face of my First Communion Timex
clicks every second left.
Green sycamore leaves demur—
the breeze chants—
their thousand upon thousand
swaying silhouettes strewn backlit
by sun across the blackboard.

Ott walks in.
Sister Anne Francis wiggles,
removes her pince-nez,

launches to her feet—
her beau just scaled the trellis—
fawning to black his brogans
with her tongue; her wedding band
to her cheek as she whispers, *Father*,
opens a drawer in her fantastic desk,
and hands him my report card.

When Ott looks up—from my red *U*
in Conduct, poor marks in *Self-Control*,
Christian Doctrine, and *Effort*—
and opens his mouth
to describe the griddle in Purgatory,
his teeth are red from breakfast borscht.
Jesus, on His crux, above the alphabet,
kites down and joins me as I float
out the window and scatter
for summer with the crows.

Cici's

Sun spills through the lintel.
The lone bulb sways on its wire
above the scarred cash register,
tacked with a crucifix,
behind which CiCi perches—
Jimmy Durante's silent twin—mute,
a living daguerreotype:
gray cardigan, chipped horn buttons,
striped mourning pants, colossal ears
and nose, snap-brim fedora.
Breath between his blue teeth trills in Italian.
In a glass casket lay penny candy:
Jawbreakers, Sugar Daddies,
Sputniks, Kisses, Tootsie Rolls,
Mary Janes, Fireballs.
Aquarial urns squat the counter:
pickled eggs in pink brine;
green dills, the size of river carp.
CiCi spreads his arms, palms up,
his way of asking what I desire—
though I wonder what took his tongue.
I arrange three pennies—
Lincoln's profile from his mausoleum.
The store smells of turned earth,
De Nobili smoke, the silence
of aged *paesani* and their *spettri* escorts.
In East Liberty, the dead, like the birds,
consort with the living.

Larimer Field

Before every game,
the coaches yelled, "Line up,"
and both teams,
twenty-eight Little Leaguers,
formed a skirmish, from the plate,
down the left field line
until it ended
at the cyclone fence on Lenora Street,
where the old *Abruzzese*,
who didn't speak English
and didn't know baseball, except DiMaggio,
sat on their porches and watched us play.
Behind them plummeted *Basa La Vallone*
(The Hollow), then Negley Run,
separating like a DMZ
the Harriet Tubman projects from Collins Avenue—
the Blacks from the Italians.

Slowly we combed Larimer Field—
black, hard, rolled with oil to keep down the filth—
for broken glass we dropped in our caps.
Come dark, prophets gathered,
smashed Iron City quarts, sweet Tokay,
took dope, left their needles and rubbers in shallow center.
Across the avenue listed Larimer School.
Built in 1896, Black children studied there.
My sister and I attended parochial Saints Peter and Paul,
two blocks down, beside Carnegie Library.

Playing baseball, I wasn't made to lie or quaver.
I understood the distance between bases,
mound to plate, circles and squares,
the long chalk line—blazing white,
blazing green (though Larimer Field was a cinder),

a giant diamond. Such geometry,
the glory of Old Testament, Shakespearian binaries:
fair, foul; safe, out.
Beyond the infield hovered dreamland:
the ball assumed, round-tripper,
hallucinatory, home run,
evanesced into ether,
its occultation of the moon.

In visions, I'd witnessed myself—
crouched in the box, my first at bat,
in heavy flannels, number 1, eight years old,
twenty-nine-inch Adirondack in my hands—
make the Sign of the Cross,
swing at that first good strike, and lift it
over the ancient brick wall in right,
Costa's store, Joseph Street,
beyond distant Larimer Bridge;
then float base to base,
finally crossing home, coveting
not laurels but solitude—
indemnified, debts paid, ledger spotless.
There was that kind of clarity.

But I was duped, punked, down on Larimer
(avenue of parables and epic falls from grace).
Frank Latin pitched.
I'd heard all about him:
skeletal, all the more cock-strong for it,
forty-six feet away, twelve years old—
freak speed coursing blue veins—
blue acne, mustache
of fifty black hairs.
Everybody feared him:

contorting like a headsman into his windup,
over the top, thunderbolt, guillotine,
devouring, decapitating, himself
as he fired—like Juan Marichal,
who would one day lay open
John Roseboro's skull with a baseball bat.

On its axis of red seams,
the pristine white Rawlings
whirled at my head, faster
than anything I'd ever seen—
meant to assassinate, then and there,
what I would later record:
how it all started that May night,
1962, on Larimer Field.
Latin burned by me three fastballs
auguring every harrow to come—
punched out without even cutting.
The twentieth century coursed in on lightning
echoed in Allen Grasso's catcher's mitt.

Levitical Bucky Williams—
plate umpire, Negro League Star,
union millwright, who worked with my dad
at Edgar Thomson Steel—threw up his fist
for the third time, keening
as if from a pulpit in the voice
of Saint Benedict the Moor.
I turned to him in disbelief—
blue blouse, chest protector,
his indicator ticking the trinity of strikes,
pig iron glare through his barred mask.

I didn't know if I should thank him.
Wasn't someone always nattering
What do you say? What do you say?
After having the living shit
beat out of me by Sister Geralda,
I was drilled to peel off her table,
turn, and say, "Thank you, Sister."

Shrovetide

On a late Friday in Lent,
I hold the flashlight

after my father,
the parish janitor,

throws the main rocker,
and cuts off the juice,

while he builds new
outlets behind the altar.

Statues of Peter,
jangling his brace of keys;

and Paul, sword unsheathed—
even Jesus on the Crucifix,

His alcove of gold—
shrive purple until Easter.

I train the beam
on my father's hands—

the dangerous knife,
his big calloused thumb

against which he slices
shiny electrical tape—

inside the nave wall:
the red wire, the black wire—

This is what you do /
This is what you don't do.

Taking It Back

Two weeks past Epiphany,
well into the new semester,
Andrew Minerva transferred
to Saints Peter and Paul—

more beautiful than any girl in class:
blue eyes, soft wavy hair, skin
the color of late wheat.
The nuns said he was *negro*,

perhaps Mexican. Or Oriental—
a cut above *negro*, I'd heard it said.
I found his silence haughty:
his utter disdain for approval,

his refusal to acknowledge
anything at all different about him.
Tall, muscled, he'd failed a grade,
flunked, maybe two.

He stumbled when made to read.
His teeth were white as the chalice veil;
and when he dreamily smiled,
he drifted farther from the rest of us—

as if sheer beauty shielded inadequacy.
Yet there was power in his ennui.
Unmoved even by baseball,
he cared for nothing,

and I suppose I hated him for it.
He sat in front of me. All day
I stared at his curls and threadbare shoulders,
wondering what it might be like to fight him.

One day he turned in his seat—
and said, *Your dad's bald* (which he was).
I called him *nigger,*
something else I'd heard—in my home

and habitually on the street; though,
again, the nuns schooled us to say *negro.*
I knew I had done something terrible,
beyond sin, to Andrew—

worse than suckering him or oathing *fuck.*
He marched to the front of the room and tattled.
It couldn't have been Sister Thomasine—
too much of an animal to have suggested dialogue,

nor Miss Manso, the pretty lay teacher—
because we all met that Sunday after High Mass,
at the convent, to discuss what had happened:
my father, I, Andrew, and Sister Anne Francis.

That's who it must have been:
treacherous Anne Francis.
This would have been difficult for my dad.
He didn't like to talk about how he felt

or peer too deeply into things, unless alone,
though he suffered nuns well,
and they idolized him. Church usher,
member of the Holy Name Society,

the will and zeal of a cheery Trappist,
he drove them to visit their aged comrades
at the Mother House in the country
and built a window box on the fire escape

for our class geraniums.
My mother sewed the satin pillow laced with pearls
upon which Mary's May crown rested.
Mother hated the nuns: their beastly looks

and savage piety. They hated her too:
she out-savaged them without a whit of piety.
That might explain her leaving that Sunday up to my dad,
or maybe he suggested she stay home,

or she just didn't want to go to church.
We talked about the bad word I'd let slip out.
Sister said she knew I really hadn't meant it.
Would I take it back?

My father looked at me.
He wanted to get the hell out
of that dark convent foyer,
its faded inquisitorial stained glass.

I took back the word,
but words can never be taken back.
Then Andrew, all alone, and I shook hands.
I told him I was sorry.

Sister explained there was nothing
at all tragic about being bald.
Priests were: Father Petrogallo, Saints
Anthony and Francis, friars and monks;

their shaved tonsures symbolized haloes.
That's when I began to get sick
and wish my mother were there
to make a scene and put a stop to it all.

Anne Francis: the hubris of Lucifer.
Priests are bald; saints are bald.
What careless things to say to a boy
who knows he's bad, bound for hell.

I wanted to bash beautiful Andrew's head in—
because I loved him,
because of what I had called him,
because he smiled and remained silent.

Strike

My grandfather Luigi
sat on CiCi's stone threshold,
waiting for my grandmother

Suzanne, after his stroke.
Stroke is kith to *strike*—
a measure in baseball,

a way of keeping time in a game
that shuns the temporal.
My father *strikes:*

almost a year in '49 and into '50—
when my sister, Marie, was born;
116 days in 1959,

when I was in first grade.
Stroke: a slash in Sister Star's
black ledger; a backhand;

swimming through deep water;
how my mother, with her mother's
long French knife, ritually prepares

the eggplant, sets her father-tailor's
six-pound *Sad* iron—*Formicola,*
the village that whelped him,

scrolled in its handle—
upon the spool of salted eggplant,
to press from it, before frying,

water pooled crimson
in the pan
beneath the colander.

Sucker Punch

I didn't know why Talese was looking for me. All I knew was that it was a serious thing, that I had somehow insulted him, and the matter required redress. I'd expected him for days and was half-relieved to see him pimp toward me through a corridor of students, uniformed in blazers and jumpers, ravenous to see what might happen, hurrying to get out of his way.

Talese and I had known each other our entire lives and had always treated each other with affection and respect. I thought of us as friends. How had I injured him? With someone like Talese, you'd never know. He'd kill for the sake of what he'd come to think of as honor. It was 1964; honor had trickled into our blood as vengeance.

He stood in front of me. Neither of us said a word. I stared into his wild blue eyes—mongrel mouth, fountain of black hair, olive skin. Exquisite as Our Lady of Guadalupe. We studied each other. Everyone watched. I contemplated hitting him first and let myself smile. He smiled in return.

The lone, self-unfruitful plum tree on the chapel lawn trembled; oval, pale-pink blossoms lifted from its twigs.

The Angelus sounded from the belfry: *Behold the handmaid of the Lord; be it unto me according to thy word.*

Talese punched me in the face—on the lower jaw, close to my earlobe.

The utter unlikelihood of it all: that I neither flinched nor budged but continued to gaze without anger or fear into his face; that he continued to gaze back at me; that not only had I survived but was enlarged; that in the settling of this thing I had never understood, yet in which I had been complicit, Talese had made me happy.

As canon law required, we then knelt in the stone schoolyard and prayed.

Excommunication

Quarantined with Father Ott
in his haunted box, I'm a fool

to have trusted him
with my cherished mortal sins—

hardly lost on me the royal irony
that his Jesuit vows forbid a girl,

any girl—anyone, anywhere.
His treble God-the-Father bass

behind the cribble booms:
You are in the power of Satan,

on the express to Hades—so thunderously
the crazed Calabrese widows,

twisted in rosaries, loafing in the nave,
nattering novenas, *squilibrata*

in preparation for the Second Coming,
fall into a frenzy of crossing themselves,

then dash from the church
to chain-smoke in the Lenten blizzard.

In labored soughs, like a bellows, Ott fumes.
Impatient for me to thank him,

and get the hell out, he fiddles
with his black Zippo:

metallic creak of its hoisted hood,
snap of its descent.

Then the scent of lighter fluid
as he flicks the flywheel—

and sparks from the flint
afford enough light to make him out,

inches from my face,
through the confessional scrim:

boozy potato nose, fey pooching lips,
stench and shade of claret, magenta stole,

white hair, licked, slick as a possum,
the cigarette, for which he's famished,

already nocked
between his consecrated fingers.

The Cellar

When my sister talked to boys on the phone,
she stretched the cord down the cellar stairs
into the dark and whispered.

My parents didn't like her down there, barefoot
on cold concrete, without a light,
talking to a boy. We had to pretend

nothing at all odd about it—
supper on the table, sacramental
supper, the sacred daily rite

of our commingled lives interrupted.
We couldn't even mention Marie
in the cellar, exchanging on the phone

whatever it might have been, at that moment,
with a nameless boy.
Everything had to be as if it weren't happening;

that was how one got through things.
My parents would have punished me
had they known what I was thinking.

I was not at all curious about them.
But I often wondered about Marie,
sixteen, 1966: Johnson's first term

after the assassination,
the year I started remembering
with dreadful precision.

My father taught her to drive
our blue Belair. Riding shotgun,
I adored that Chevy, my sister behind the wheel,

windows down, her long hair blowing.
I punched radio buttons, station to station,
lashing music over us, like I was typing her story,

as she sang from memory, and I mumbled.
Without even realizing, she shaved the hairpin
on Mellon Terrace while I held my breath

and tried to get it all down with speed
and truth before 1967 showed up
and she left for college at Slippery Rock.

I loved her secret life,
living through all she yearned for alone,
in the cellar: with the coal furnace,

copper pipes weaving in and out
of the ancient rafters that held up the house,
my father's tools, our sleds,

shelves of empty jars, canned hams,
fruit cocktail—statues and crucifixes
my mother thought a little much for upstairs.

In her nightgown, Mother washed clothes
down there, where my father shaved,
our retreat when we craved solitude,

in its very center a drain
that flowed to the city sewer,
then the Allegheny, west on the Ohio,

all the way to California.
Marie ascended to us, from the cellar,
changed, all of us changed.

What had she and that boy talked of?
We made the Sign of the Cross,
said Grace, and ate supper.

Jeanne-Marie

I swore never to lose the summer night
on Chatham's dripping green campus
when I and Jeanne-Marie,
an exchange from Chantilly

I'd a mere semester to adore,
stumbled from the soft rain
into the ancient gym,
as Harry Chapin warmed the first chords

of "Taxi," an anthem on the art
of losing I listened to, eyes closed,
like I was that loner hack, poor Harry—
the fare he'd just picked up,

unbelievably, his lost love, Sue—
and heartbreak not sordid
but something to crave.
On the blessed front end

of all that had been foretold,
I lived in *before,* as we all must,
as long as afforded
by karma, fate, or grace,

difficult as it is to discern
the beginning from the end.
We sat the floor half-court
in the jump circle:

her pious face, black boots,
black hair, beret, black dress
—black eyes. Drastic overbite,
teeth milk glass–white—

Luna moth skin, too-red lipstick,
macramé. Two names—*Jeanne
Marie*—she tutored me to say.
Melodramatic wet night, 1973,

marijuana wafted from the garden.
Wistful Harry—makeshift stage
beneath the backboard, its frilly net
hung over his head—

finally took it all out on his Martin,
lick-on-lick-hair-shirt ferocity—
all the love he'd ever on this earth reckoned
left to conceit "in the back of the Dodge."

I'd not lost anything yet—
not this French farmgirl I worshipped.
That it might drip light,
the half-sturgeon moon,

thralled through the bashful rain
to its station above the bell tower.
The college runners, in purple satin singlets,
appeared from afar, skimmed the lawns,

passed the quad fountain, and were upon us
the signature moment Harry's bass guitarist,
Big John Wallace,
prodigious head of hair and beard,

like a "wild man, wizard,"
rose above the band—
his colossal shadow, a portent,
against the plank walls—

and keened, *Over 'til my time,*
runs out, like the Angel Gabriel
unlatching his wings
at the Annunciation.

The meter ticked, that cruel twenty—
the image stays with me—
scrolled in Harry's pocket...
I held Jeanne-Marie's hand.

As they ran by, the runners turned
in rapture toward the gym.

PART III

Manovale

> He accepted that work was part of a man's hard fate; if all men did that, there just might be some justice in this world.
>
> —Cesare Pavese, "Smokers of Paper"

No Use Kicking

Each night over supper, in the house on Mellon,
I learned from my parents what work is.
Our street was named for one of the families
that owned Pittsburgh,
even a cathedral in East Liberty:
Andrew Mellon and his big white mustache
peered from the purple three-cent stamp.

The Mellon Street house was the only house
my parents purchased, in 1964,
for $12,000 dollars, after living as newlyweds
with Aunt Lu and Uncle Artie, then renting
their first seventeen years of marriage.
They had a dollar and a half between them
when they left the lawyer at closing.

Still deranged by the Depression,
they whispered, "the war,"
as if it'd been yesterday,
though the new war brewed in the Gulf of Tonkin
and goggled Barry Goldwater gaped
like a madman from our Zenith.
We were Democrats, unionists:
United Steelworkers,
Garment Workers of America.

My mother, still in her pretty cream blouse,
with the jabot, jade pin in its floret knot,
at her throat, to hide the thyroid scar,
railed against the *gavone* tailors and pressers—
Ziggy Barone, slicker, dandy,
his *bastone* and silk scarf, greenhorn—
knocking down, writing numbers,
bootlegging with the hophead porters in Will Call,

while she and Fausta Nocce, Chickie Scarano,
Elsie Cestra, all those *girls,* hunched
like *stracciona*—treated like *puttana*—
in rows of pounding secondhand Singers
in Sears and Roebuck cellar sweatshop.

My father had already cleaned up in the basement—
from his fiery world on the open hearth:
heats, ladles, Bessemers, blast furnaces,
pig iron, coke, slag, ore, melts—
and washed his work fatigues
in the hand-crank wringer Speed Queen.
His asbestos jumpsuit choked from a copper pipe.
He smiled and whistled smoke from his Camel
toward my mother, asleep on her arms,
at her end of the table.
"No use kicking," he liked to say.
Faccia contenta: fall to your knees,
make the face of contentment.

I said to myself, *This is what work is:*
busting your ass, eating shit,
punching in, punching out,
grudging breaks, permission to piss,
kissing someone's ass every minute;
foremen, straw bosses, scabs;
insult, injury, at best boring, cruel;
fatica so bewildering it steals your soul;
but never, *God help you,* breach a picket.

Catharsis

After wrestling practice, I wait at Fifth & Neville
for the 71 Negley—still downtown,

crawling along frozen rivers a rush-hour blizzard.
Stuffed in my gym bag are stinking sweats and Sophocles.

The second day of Lent—so cold spit freezes
when it strikes the telephone pole—

church sanctuaries disguise in purple,
the Resurrection so distant, it seems impossible.

Across the avenue beckons Cathedral Pharmacy,
forbidden, blinding as Hopper:

buttered toast, lemon Cokes, a blonde candy striper,
the danger of slipping through the portal of regret

into the maudlin ache for Heaven.
Hopper is dead not quite a year,

though I've not heard of him, not yet,
nor Neal Cassady, gone too, just days before,

in the icy gall of February,
a month of no expectation for starvelings—

just the spit jar and bum bracket seed
with a veiny cock-strong psycho in the tournament.

Packed with straphangers, cigarettes and slush,
the bus finally wheezes to the curb.

A few bundled stiffs tumble out the center doors.
I grab a strap and dangle.

Down to one lane, we lurch meter by meter,
swaying against one another.

Our faces glare back at us in the long window:
forgettery, sacrilegious fatigue,

the illusion a home awaits.
Salt crews sidle in with slag.

Lorry chains ring.
After an hour, I score a seat,

open my book to what happens
when the prideful piss off God—

an exam tomorrow on Aristotelian tragedy,
then the match: stripped, on a frigid scale,

pleading with God I make weight
in a moldy Southside locker room.

Facing me sleeps a woman:
lipstick, earrings, gold pin on her heavy red coat,

purse locked in her elbow,
black high-heeled boots toggled to the ankle—

this apparition: my mother,
fighting to wake in the preternatural light,

snow—petals of it, wet white—
fleecing behind her the lonesome night.

How like her: here all along since boarding
two hours earlier under Kaufmann's clock

after ten hours in a basement tailor shop,
chained to a sewing machine.

When she opens her eyes, she doesn't know where she is.
The gauzy night impersonates dream.

Finally, she smiles and pats the empty seat beside her.
The last two—the bus skids to its final stop—

we slash home through drifts along the reservoir.
Ducks paddle the sky.

Giuseppe Moretti's 1896 bronze statues—
naked women—gate piers at the threshold

of Highland Park, in flimsy shawls
of rime, lift torches.

Wisdom

Secreted in my gums,
five of my milk teeth
from infancy remain,
and I have four impacted third molars—
wisdom teeth, so-called
as they arrive uselessly late,
nothing but trouble,
when you've supposedly the brains
of an adult, yet still freaked by thunder.
They all have to go—in the hospital,
like an operation. Easy enough.
Everyone has it done—in and out.
Your face swells, discolors a few days.
A couple aspirin, then back to the fray.
Wheeled to the theater, suddenly
bathed in surgical lamps, and under;
then back in my room,
coming to, foggy, gray forenoon
twitching through Venetian blinds,
an IV in my arm, the line
to the withered bag dangling from its tree.
My dad, at the foot of the bed, peers down at me.
My mother, in good clothes, holds my hand.
Perhaps I am dying—all this gravity.
Blinding alabaster, cap to oxfords,
a nurse flashes in, removes the IV,
commands, "Let's get you out of here,
but first you have to pee."
A lone bud of blood blooms from the puncture.
My father leads me, wobbly,
in my scant paisley dress, to the toilet.
I lift its hem, try and try.
He flicks on the sink's spigot
as he had when I staggered, a wee boy,

through nightmare to my parents' bed,
too groggy to shake hell from my head,
too petrified to pee. He'd carry me
to the bathroom, steady me over the bowl,
as we listened to the running faucet
divine the well in me. After a spell,
like a miracle—the sound of water
conjures water—the river rife
within us all began to flow.

Shouldering It

The summer I worked construction,
it was Whitman—
not a bricklayer,
but a common laborer like I,

a *manovale*—
who told me to stay in school,
that once I hit his age,
I'd rue on my shoulder the hod

he'd humped every day
since dropping out
at seventeen in '45 to invade Japan—
forsaking a ride at fullback

awaiting him at Lincoln.
But we dropped *Little Boy* and *Fat Man*
on Hiroshima and Nagasaki.
War ended, and Whit

signed on with this outfit.
In a year, he married.
At twenty-one, three kids.
By thirty, two more.

Five mouths to feed, he moonlighted
weekends humping Sheetrock
for the new skyscraper downtown.
His wife cleaned houses and changed diapers

at a day care across the river.
They got everywhere by jitney and trolley.
He listened to WAMO, the Black station,
during lunch on his transistor:

Ahmad Jamal and Sweet Pea Strayhorn.
All that mattered, he swore, was family,
one buck more than you could spend,
and a decent pair of shoes.

I fathomed his life through books:
Tolstoy's peasants,
colliers in *Sons and Lovers*.
I romanticized my toil in ways only a boy can:

men's work in the sun and dirt, bare chested.
But after the first day, I knew
I wasn't worth a damn.
Whit gave me gloves—he wore none—

to baby my soft hands.
He taught me to drink water.
One day, I referred to sumac
hovering the scaffold as *foliage*

and the whole site cracked up.
Whit was right.
I was merely passing through,
a college kid on my way out of Pittsburgh,

out of steel—where exactly I didn't know.
I'd learned in class that destination
is mere illusion, a construct
mired between Marx and Freud.

The only thing I knew for certain
was what I couldn't stomach—
and that was most everything.
Each workday, I prayed for a rainout,

that I be spared, to read of the *fellaheen*,
the *proles*, my ancestors packed in steerage
on the shivering Atlantic,
their heads bloodied for a pittance,

so someday I'd be paid to study them.
The men I worked with preferred suffering
to losing eight hours pay to weather.
This was no union shop, no OSHA, no hard hat,

just an hourly wage; and your name, please God,
on the list every morning when you punched in,
thermos and lunch bucket, at 6:30.
They were making ends meet:

not two nickels to rub together;
not a pot to piss in;
a crust of bread was a crust of bread.
They bore witness to the value of a dollar:

Faulkner's *old thrill and ... old despair*
of a penny more or less.
That summer, Whitman was forty-seven—
twenty-four years younger than I am now—

his hair the color of fresh mortar;
eyes wet gray too, seared
with what could have only been love,
but something even more devastating.

Everyone seemed old then—and I wonder
what I might have looked like,
if they even noticed my shuffling
among them, on my shoulder

the cumbrous hod, quaking
with my longing and their grief;
genuflecting to the bricklayers
kneeling on calloused knees

and stabbing out cigarettes
in their mortarboards
as they troweled the next course,
and the next, into the wall,

ascended the scaffold,
and beckoned Whitman to stock them.
He spaded 100 pounds of mortar into a hod,
canted 100 pounds of brick into another,

heaved them to his shoulders
and made for the sky:
three stories, to the deadly gables,
on shaky two-by-twelves—

sluice from the dripping wedges
striped his naked back—
into the sun, the calling crows,
the hushed thrall of ether.

Basic Oxygen

> Basic oxygen process (BOP), a steelmaking method in which pure oxygen is blown into a bath of molten blast-furnace iron and scrap. The oxygen initiates a series of intensively exothermic (heat-releasing) reactions, including the oxidation of such impurities as carbon, silicon, phosphorus, and manganese.
>
> —*Encyclopedia Britannica*

My father left me his hardhat
and silver belt buckle
(*B.O.P.*—the BOP Shop—
in relief against a blue field);
his union and social security cards;
a Polaroid of his retirement party
in the maintenance shack—
a dingy block pillbox with a coffee urn,
caged bar of fluorescent lights,
and wall clock, 3:00 p.m. straight up:

He slices a sheet cake:
a frosted crucible of white heat;
torrents of smoke and fire; barges
scudding coal up the swollen Ohio;
bridges, like phosphorescent necklaces,
draping black water; *Joe* ladled
beneath a chocolate blast furnace.
He and his smiling comrades
wear asbestos, and safety goggles.

Their living names and phone numbers—
blowtorched in my father's cuneiform
into the tiny brown notebook (also left to me)
he carried but never wrote in—
not like we say *wrote in:*

no leisure introspection—
my father's mood,
slant of light / cast of sky / how he felt.

I wonder if anyone ever asked how he felt.
He would have answered with a smooth
clause of smoke from his Camel:
What does that have to do with anything?
He had to punch in, make time / make a buck.
He wore a watch to avoid being docked.

My father had plenty to write about:

> *Domenico Giuseppe*
> *immigrant famiglia*
> *Manfredonia Puglia*
> *mother dead childbirth*
> *1920 five years old*
> *rakehell blacksmith father*
> *seven brothers sisters*
> *abandoned*
> *mauled by dog*
> *hungry stole pie*
> *Thorn Hill*
> *quit school*
> *Depression War*
> *married Rose two kids*
> *a roof milk bread shoes*
> *dead man's shift*
> *strikes layoffs*
> *moonlighting*

What else was there to say?
Why put it on paper?
He didn't have all day.
He made steel: direct, paratactic—

nouns, verbs, urgent syntax,
(all caps, exclusively graphite)—
code more than alphabet:
slashes, circles, glyphs;
rebar, slag and ingots
soldered into syllables—
essential names and numbers,
the ghosts of millwrights
murmuring in brackish
carp water lapping
broken glass, rusty pylons.

And that final entry
on the notebook's last three lines
(a fifty tucked in the pages):
DONT FEEL BAD
A LITTLE SOMETHING
LOTS LOVE DAD

PART IV
Aspettare

I'll tell you what I hate about writing. Finishing it. It comes to an end. You can't come forever. When I'm finished, I can't remember what it was like inside the doing. I can't remember.

—Frank Lentricchia, *The Edge of Night*

The Raccoon

Like an old Italian man,
wobbling from too much wine,
lost on his way home from bocce,
he strayed into our yard—
confused, overdressed in black
overcoat and banded gray fedora,
the gamy smell of De Nobili cigars.

When I opened the front door, he turned.
He'd lost an eye a long time ago.
He seemed to lift a hand:
Perhaps a very small vino?
Sweating, clearly sick,
he struggled to stand.

I thought it rabies.
But it was distemper,
the animal control officer
explained. Young, lovely,
he apologized for what he had to do.

The raccoon—tail soaked, lusterless, rings faded—
had scrabbled into the *basilico*,
shivering on the stone wall that grottoed
the weathered statue of the Madonna
in a bed of Easter lilies abloom.

The young man placed the cage
in the shade of the dogwood.
He was gentle with the snare pole.
Out of kindness, he said:
Sometimes they can be cured.
The raccoon watched fearlessly—
a station of the cross.

When I was very little, my grandfather,
Compadre Paolo, ate Sunday dinner with us.
He twirled his pasta against a soup spoon.
The way he lifted his hand:
More bread, more wine.
But he used that hand, as well, for *No More.*
Aspettare, he'd growl. Wait!
His voice: iron rust. Bone on bone.
What was he waiting for?
He'd had enough.
He wanted to disappear.

The raccoon bowed,
offered himself,
surrendered to the halo.

Mount Carmel

A black crucifix
towers the hill

above the first tombs
hacked into Mount Carmel.

Its alabaster Christ
eyes His vast plat of Italians.

Their outlandish names
dance like tarantulas.

The sky is Mary blue,
winter sun her halo.

Your mother vowed—
with relish, for effect,

when the future darkened conversation—
she'd lie here one day;

and here, this day, you wander,
searching for her and your father

who never threatened to die.
Like Saint Anthony,

he could turn up anything.
Your mother never lost a button.

You don't come often,
yet when you do,

you can't find them—
by simply twisting the doorknob

and there they doze,
in the living room,

Mass on television,
the streets to Sacred Heart too icy.

You cannot lift the phone,
make sure they're settled for the night,

have what they need until daylight;
nor ask the neighbors, here, as well,

at your feet, to look in on them.
Disonore:

to understand perfectly
your mother and father

repose two meters beneath the earth
you tread, and you can't find them—

their very names you dictated
for the chisel (your name)

on the vanished ledger stone.
Forbidden to call out,

as you pace above them,
what must they think

of your shambling,
your muddy cuffs?

Extreme Unction

My mother threatened life-long to die
and was finally making good on it.
Perhaps, all along, that *I'll be dead* rag
had been a ploy to live past eighty-five.

The rookie Jesuit played Extreme Unction
like a Jerry Lewis schtick—
even looked like him: bucked teeth,
goofy black glasses, deranged stare,

spiky Sputnik hair. He snurgled
and mugged, haplessly dear, inquiring:
How is everyone? Where was I?
Patting himself down for his stole

and breviary, fumbling the Eucharist,
for which my mother was too far gone,
he couldn't seem to find anything.
Not the least bit grave, which suited me—

I would've wanted to punch
a *gravitas* man of God—
he dubbed this sacrament
The Anointing of the Sick,

which doesn't sound so bad,
more like medicine than farewell,
counter to the *Last Rites'* final knell,
How comforting that Mother ended up

with a comedian as her final confessor.
Just a kid out of seminary
in a bum spot (his first gig),
after each malapropism

and muddle through the office,
he looked to me for approval—
like *How am I doing?*
My mother was in and out,

conscious in that spooky
liminal way of dying.
Her hair, of which she was fiercely proprietary,
spread the pillow—not *done*

as usual by rote at La Bellissima.
She would have never permitted
my touching it—taboo—as I did,
for the first time since a baby.

Surely this will rouse her, I thought.
Soft wavy white, it sparkled
against the coral cloudbank
at the window above the headboard—

not quite dusk, the last day of August.
I held her hand with my other
and waited for the dig:
I had to die for you to hold my hand.

She had ceased talking—
this time she meant it—
would never again open her pretty brown eyes
but smiled when I explained my dad,

notorious for his sweet tooth,
had whisked the kids off for ice cream.
The pamphlet the social worker had given him,
on how to let go, sat on the table

next to his chair at her bedside—
he had started it and set it aside—
among my mother's prescription bottles,
encircled by chaplets; her missal

of litanies to the Blessed Mother,
her namesake; needle, thread,
thimble, pearl-handled basting knife;
a baby quilt she'd been piecing.

The Jesuit anointed her hands
and forehead with chrism,
made over her the Sign of the Cross,
and shook upon her his aspergillum,

soaking me as well with holy water.
In the pretty light, it prismed her face.
"Mother," I whispered.
The Jesuit tripped a few steps

and put his arm around me.
"She can't hear you," he said gently
and pulled me close.
I was grateful for his good heart,

his fledgling Roman collar.
But he didn't know my mother, about to depart
(though—she'd made up her mind—
not until my dad returned),

yet still canny enough to take in
this final farce, and I imagined her,
even as she sailed off, smart-ass till the end,
cracking up as she mimicked him.

Right Guard

As he aged, my father dwindled,
not in stature—though he grew smaller
as elders must—but rather in estate.
He never required much,

insisted on giving things away.
What am I going to do with all this?
Suddenly I had his shirt,
wristwatch, hammer and plane—

his car keys and driver's license
when the time came. I arrived,
the night of his death,
and stole a moment alone in his room

at The Pines, a name too green
and pulsing, filled with trees—
near infuriating—for a tomb.
My mother had died a year earlier.

To save money to pass along to me
and my sister, my father requested
a move to an efficiency—a monk's cell.
At heart, he was an ascetic.

I sat on the edge of his small bed,
where he'd perched that morning—
September 3,
his 59th wedding anniversary,

my mother gone a year—to quell his vertigo,
hands folded, his dawn office,
before launching his day.
He witnessed the first rind

of sabbath sun cross the sash.
Song sparrows chanted *Asperges me*.
Then, prepared, he rose.
I stood and paced behind his shade,

gauging where, in the modest span
between his bedclothes and coffeepot,
he decided to join my mother—
privately, no announcement, illness,

deathwatch. No priest.
The attention would have embarrassed him.
His only flourish was the white pressed
handkerchief on him at all times.

Perhaps he glimpsed his *fetch*
or, responsive to my mother's whims,
her beckoning;
or his own mother, whom, at five,

he'd lost to childbirth.
Given neither to signs nor bodement,
never mysterious, but like us all
who parse life step by step,

my father kept a secret life
he alone entered—nothing terrible,
or even curious—a silent chamber
he had the wisdom, the courage,

to leave locked, the key hidden—
though he had little use for metaphor.
A millwright, a steelman,
he discovered the ladled heat,

and molten pour, the union shop,
a practice he abided and died for.
What was there left of his to take?
He'd already given me everything.

I wandered into the tiny bathroom.
Stationed on the shelf above the sink
stood a can of Right Guard,
the only deodorant my dad used—

Original, of course, *Sport:*
the logo stick figure, in full throttle,
bolting from the blocks.
I grabbed it and pressed the actuator.

The valve hissed and hung a familiar
incensed mist. Out of it,
like a genie summoned from its lamp,
appeared my father.

The First Time They Forget

You love them all the more
for the worry: the kettle
melting on the eye;
they've strayed too far
in the automobile
you'll inevitably take away
and wrecked; the phone
out of order; they've fallen—
on the floor, dead; heatstroke;
they nap; maybe just busy,
they'll ring later.
But how could they
have forgotten
their parts in this day,
half a century ago:
the long gestation and rush
that summer dawn to the hospital,
your father pacing the solarium,
Camel after Camel,
you and your mother
astonished at finally meeting
through a mirror placed at her heels?
When it's unbearable, you ring.
At your voice, they realize, abashed,
and you hate yourself,
still a needy child,
for your lies of reassurance—
No big deal; please don't worry about it—
as if it's not your birthday,
your call just a check-in,
not the very last of one thing
and the onset of another.

A Pittsburgh Bakery in Winter

Into Prantl's, on Walnut Street,
through the sudden scrim of snow,

an ancient white-haired couple hovers.
Dusk of Pittsburgh frigid winter,

enough to freeze the rivers,
after hours of rare, exquisite sun,

now vanished for another score of days,
yet still firing in the icicles

knifed from the bakery awning—
the hour the very old appear to fetch sweets

swathed in silver tissue laid
in white boxes latched with string.

The woman holds the man's arm.
He wears a gold cap,

she a gold scarf, like a babushka,
about her head—their kind faces

scrubbed clean by the twentieth century.
So small, they smile, so aged,

almost frightening, they pluck numbers
and enter the long queue.

The bakery is warm, blinding,
glass cases of cream puffs, éclairs,

lady locks, napoleons,
French doughnuts, meringue—

the glory of unbridled desire,
confections of the living.

Katy

After the first plane,
Katy phoned her brother.
She was safe, in *another* building.

They were evacuating.
DJ thought she had said *the other building*—
the South Tower—crashed into

by United Flight 175 at 9:03,
moments after the line went dead.
That's all Katy's mother, my sister,

Marie, could tell me when I called.
All we had to cling to:
a single syllable, separating *another*

from *other*, negligible, mere nuance;
but, in this case, the difference
between escape and incineration—

a seam notched for her in the secret ether,
should she stumble into it,
to pass through unharmed.

To cast wider our search,
Marie and I tuned to different networks,
watching for Katy among the fleeing hordes.

They had talked the night before
about what she'd wear to her client meeting:
brown suit, black bag; her black hair

shorter since last I'd seen her.
All day I peered into the TV—punching
the cordless: Katy's office, home, cell,

office, home, cell, over and over—scanning
faces unraveling diabolically
like smoldering newsreels, smeared

with hallucinatory smoke and ash.
They came in ranks, wave upon wave,
leagued across the avenues:

the diaspora into John's Apocalypse.
Those still on their feet staggered.
Others lay in the street snarled

in coils of writhing fire hose.
The firmament had been napalmed:
orange plumed, spooled black. Volcanic stench.

Somewhere beyond the screen,
inside that television from which we all, that day,
received, like communion, the new covenant,

for all time, hid my niece in her brown suit
and new haircut, her purse—outfitted
for her seventh day in Manhattan,

her fourth day at the World Financial Center,
six days past her 22nd birthday.
I would spy her, coax her back to us

through the TV's lurid circuitry
into my living room. Our perfect girl,
my princess—she had lost her shoes—

wandering the skewered heart of the future—
finally arrived, black hooded, afire,
eerily mute—toward the Upper East Side:

a bus, a shared cab with an old man
who befriended her, then barefoot blocks
and blocks to her apartment on 89th Street,

where she dialed her parents and announced
with the sacrificial modesty of saints
that she had made it home.

Wedding Soup

(For Russel Benko)

Russel calls from his apartment in Pittsburgh—
gravelly bull moose barrel laugh.
He's watching golf on TV
and making wedding soup for Joe Costanzo.

This cook Russel is new to me,
this tenderness—his love for Joe,
who's having a rough time. As kids,
they met every day at the corner

of Deely and Beehner, then walked
to school at St. Rosalia's.
This soup means everything:
the imported *pastina;*

Russel's preference for escarole,
though spinach or endive will do.
The garlic. Fresh stock.
He reveals his secret with gravity:

this much veal in your meatballs—
no larger, *remember,*
than a cocktail onion.
I'd once thought wedding soup

celebratory, even holy—
the sacrament of matrimony.
But the name originates
from *minestra maritata:*

Married soup. "Married"
because of the tryst of flavors.
We get around to football senior year,
losing to North

in the Catholic League Championship;
and conclude, *Fuck it,* as we do at dead ends
about what went wrong half a century ago.
You wouldn't have pegged

big raucous Russel for a punter,
not the maestro, the da Vinci, of punters:
contemplative, the balletic ritual
and preen as he conjured

the long snap from center. Alone,
unprotected, yards from scrimmage—
they were coming to take his head off—
he refused to hurry:

laid the ball, laces up, on the night,
then kicked it over the lights
of Southside Stadium, beyond
the boom cranes on the river Mon,

—where it hung, spiraling,
the waxing gibbous moon.
Smoky East Carson St. clouds split.
People were struck dumb.

Ubi Sunt

> A poetic motif emphasizing the transitory nature of youth, life, and beauty.
>
> —*Collins English Dictionary*

In the bottom-left corner of Pennsylvania,
along the brindle Monongahela,
and a string of spent coal hamlets
that played out in the town of California,
I walked on—a freshman pole vaulter,
at the small state college.

For a sole season was I a Vulcan,
fire-god, red and black silks and singlet—
more smolder, smoke, than burn—
the sputtering script of my life
as an athlete I'd authored to the bitter end.

Often, I fouled at the first height,
scratching the forbidden crossbar,
then pitched with it—
scrubbed from the board—
into the bloated Cloud Nine pit.
My name appeared but once
in the *Cal Times*—
misspelled, of course.

Yet the few riffs of romance remain:
the occasions I did clear the ether and score,
the formal feeling of donning the colors,
prancing the runway for the jump;
thumbing frigid to campus from practice
every Appalachian eve on California Road;
nocturnal bus treks in a sprung Bluebird
to spooky locker rooms
in West Virginia and central PA.

Through the night, I stacked the turntable
six deep with LPs. One by one,
they dropped to the needle: *After the Gold Rush,*
John Barleycorn Must Die, Déjà Vu,
Tea for the Tillerman, Blue,
The Low Spark of High-Heeled Boys.
I posted my first benighted lyrics,
based on despair I'd yet to notch,
to the *New Yorker* (I wish I were kidding)—
on lined loose-leaf, in prim penmanship,
untyped, no SASE—certain I'd vouchsafed
in wholly new ways ache and yearn
(*ubi sunt,* a literary term I'd acquired
in American Literature), and its editors
would concur with hosannas,
rather than laugh, which they must have done.

Mornings, I ran the graveyard before class;
memorized "Sinners in the Hands of an Angry God,"
undone by Faith's ribbons in "Young Goodman Brown."
I spied Claggart's "black blood"
in the shower grout and sidewalk cracks.
How I loved the symbol—
stammering Billy, dangling
in white from the yardarm.

I hopped a Monongahela Railway
freighter hauling coal upriver
and clung till my hands numbed
to a rusty ladder spined up the caboose.
White birds sailed over fraught water.
The moon rolled out of the woods
and I leapt—
ripped open in the railbed my jeans,

scarped and cindered palms,
tumbled, a little lonesome,
into the weeds, but not so bad.

Then I walked the crossties back to California,
for another all-nighter with Puritan theology,
and my dormitory of Mon Valley *droogs*
from Monessen, Donora, Belle Vernon—
their Sunshine and glue, formaldehyde,
peyote, a bushel of Downs;
Alice Cooper and long green WWII trench coats
from the Army Surplus in Charleroi,
where I purchased a machete
just before we hitchhiked home
for Christmas to fetch lottery numbers
in the Vietnam draft.

PART V

Coda

shudder and clang of steel on steel

…

a sudden silence:

—Giovanni Pascoli, "Last Dream"

Requiem for the Living

When I pray for Phil on my morning run,
as I always have, and register
a small detonation in my chest
that he is gone, I call his name

loudly enough that hoodlum crows,
of whom I'm so sentimentally fond, lift
from the towering pines, as they call back.
Dorothy Day believed prayers for the dead

help them while they were living on earth.
I don't understand this,
but Phil and Rose are together tonight.
Everything is ahead; and if I'm quiet,

for just another moment,
I'll find my hand upon the secret panel
that swings open their world,
and there they'll be—on the balcony

of their Polish Hill walk-up
on Beethoven Street.
It's April, a week from Easter.
Spring has promised not only to stay

but dazzle: green and yellow,
trees and flowers, a madhouse of birds,
so warm, Phil wears his purple shirt,
the sun in Pittsburgh a miracle.

My impulse is to barge in, interrogate them.
But this is taboo.
Absolved of the dark caprice of time,
like postulants, they plan the future.

Phil paints the sycamores,
his famous triptych of enormous oils—
studies of a mythic tree, at the entrance
of a black block tunnel, in Highland Park.

Rose's mauve batik dries on a chair,
her hair the pert yellow of pears,
skin pale as frost.
Cigarette smoke swaddles

fetal angels at their heads.
The chartreuse Allegheny
rolls toward the Monongahela.
You see it from their fire escape.

You see the gardens
the old Italian people in Bloomfield
plant on their roofs.
You see Liberty Avenue.

Steady Daylight

Today in Heaven,
my father turned 105.
Finally working steady daylight
he's got it knocked:
eight to four,
double-time-and-a-half—
no asbestos,
no shoveling slag
on the open hearth;
no depending from a boom crane,
six degrees, in sleet;
no boss—
thirteen weeks vacation annually
Kingdom Come.
The union up here takes zero shit.

Home well before dark,
traffic mellow, blue sky,
nothing but green signals;
plenty of time, once home—
perfect parking spot
right in front of the house—
to sit a minute, smoke a Camel,
sip an Iron City pony
beneath the olive and lemon trees
he planted when he first arrived—
368 days after my mother
(to celebrate their 59th anniversary).
They grow well in Heaven—
mild weather year-round,
like Puglia,
save for snow on holy days & feasts.
He shaves and showers in the cellar.

My mother has his clothes for the party
laid out on their bed:
khakis, short-sleeved
summer white shirt.

The party's at Aunt Lu's,
everybody there—at each stage
of their lives, concurrently.
Another time,
this would have struck them as outlandish.
Not now.
They were poor; they suffered.
Now they're happy.
Money's not an issue.
No one gets sick.
No one gets hurt.
The neighborhood's safe.
Everyone gets along. At all times,
they act reasonably.
Light surrounds them.
It's that kind of place.

Angels from the ether
bear platters of ravioli
from Groceria Italiano
in Bloomfield; sausage
from Joe Grasso on Larimer Avenue;
lemon ice from Moio's;
sfogliatelle from Barsotti;
Parmesan, aged for eternity;
scungilli from Umberto's Clam House
that Uncle Ralph scored from a Detroit crony;
wine from the wedding feast at Canaan.

My mother made the artichokes
and baked my dad's favorite—
egg custard pie,
every single candle: 105.

"Joe looks good," says my mother.
Says my dad, "Gimme a kiss, Rose."
With no hesitation, she dips in—
long brown hair,
brown eyes, red lipstick,
sassy '40s dress,
halo hovering like lilac.
My dad's taken to rope sandals
and straw fedora.
They're movie stars.
She sits on his lap.
He looks at his watch.
"Tomorrow's another working day," he says, and winks.

They form a conga line
and weave the rooms and halls,
up through the bedrooms,
into the attic, singing:
"Grandma's Lye Soap."
Aunt Margaret deals blackjack
at the big dining room table.
All the food is still out,
but they decide to cook again:
peppers and eggs, hot sausage.
Black Velvet, the blonde
in the black velvet dress
and pearls on its label,
turns itself in trickles

upside down
into shot glasses.
Chubby Checker on the turntable,
the kids doing The Twist.

Uncle Pippi starts with the Italian songs.
Papa twirls Aunt Theresa
in a tarantella
and, suddenly winter, it begins to snow.
Here they are, saying goodbye:
time to go home,
kissing, bundling babies,
shackling chains to cars.
My father helps his mother,
Maria Cristina Bocchiccchio,
down the steep stone stairs
to Lemington Avenue.
He's not seen her since he was five—
a hundred years (*cento anni*).
On his right arm,
his hammer arm,
is tattooed an American eagle,
arrows in its beak,
above which unfurls *Mother*.
He must've gotten it in the Army.
How could I have never asked?
Angelo stands to his knees in snow
and plays his lost violin.

The Feast of San Mauro

Dominus vobiscum: morning comes.
Six a.m., 4 degrees, sky ebon

icy velvet, sugared with stars,
a purplish moon, fracted scars

white at its rind, wind chill -23.
Plows and salt lorries grind and spray.

Hooded, masked, county road gangs
shovel atop heaps of slag.

Crimson hazards bloody black slush.
Stray buses labor Fifth Avenue:

stoned straphangers, riding home, flush
from the dead man's shift

on the open hearth, cower
in garish dawn fluorescence.

Those just beginning their turn
hunch at the stop, in exhaust,

smoking. Ramparts smolder
in the secret vaults of Heaven

where a Benedictine from Rome,
the Patron Saint of Cold, San Mauro,

who quickened the dead, peers—
at my father's shoulder, his twin—

through lacy kitchen curtains of snow.
Et cum spiritu tuo.

www.ingramcontent.com/pod-product-compliance
Lightning Source LLC
Chambersburg PA
CBHW030122170426
43198CB00009B/703